This book was compiled by Daniel Melehi
with the A.I assistance of Inventabot

<u>Dedication</u>

I hope this helps all of my wonderful
readers achieve all their goals in their
business. And I would like to thank my
wonderful wife for all of her continued
support in all my ventures.

May 7 2023

Contents

Introduction

Who is this book for?

Who is this book for?

This book is for anyone who wants to learn how to build apps using Bubble.io. Whether you are a beginner or an experienced app developer, this book will provide you with the knowledge and skills you need to create amazing apps.

If you are new to Bubble.io, this book will guide you through the process of creating your first app step by step. You will learn the basics of the platform, including how to set up your account, create a new app, and add elements to your app. You will also learn how to use Bubble.io's drag-and-drop interface to design your app's user interface, add functionality, and publish your app to the web.

If you are already familiar with Bubble.io, this book will help you take your skills to the next level. You will learn advanced techniques for building complex apps, including how to use custom JavaScript to add powerful functionality to your app. You will also learn how to optimize your app for performance, scale your app to handle millions of users, and integrate your app with other services and platforms.

This book is also for entrepreneurs, small business owners, and anyone who wants to create a successful app-based business. You will learn how to validate your app idea, find your target audience, and build a sustainable business model around your app. You will also learn how to market your app, attract users, and grow your app into a successful business.

In summary, this book is for everyone who wants to learn how to build amazing apps with Bubble.io. Whether you are a beginner or an experienced app developer, this book will provide you with the knowledge and skills you need to create successful apps that make a difference in the world.

What is Bubble.io?

Bubble.io is a web application development platform that allows anyone to create complex web applications without having to write a single line of code. It was launched in 2012 by Emmanuel Straschnov and Josh Haas, and has since become one of the most popular no-code platforms available.

At its core, Bubble.io is a visual programming language that allows users to create complex workflows, database structures, and user interfaces without having to write any code. This is achieved through a drag-and-drop interface that allows users to add and customize various elements of their application, such as buttons, forms, and data fields.

One of the key features of Bubble.io is its ability to integrate with a wide range of external services, including payment gateways, email services, and social media platforms. This makes it possible to create fully-featured web applications that can handle everything from online payments to social media sharing.

Another key feature of Bubble.io is its scalability. Because it is built using cloud technology, applications built on the platform can be easily scaled up or down depending on the needs of the user. This makes it an ideal platform for startups and small businesses that need to quickly develop and deploy web applications without worrying about server infrastructure.

Despite its many features, Bubble.io is remarkably easy to use. The platform comes with a wide range of templates and pre-built components that make it easy for even novice users to create complex applications. Additionally, the platform has a thriving community of users who are always willing to help out with any questions or problems that might arise.

All in all, Bubble.io is an incredibly powerful and versatile platform that is capable of creating complex web applications with ease. Whether you're an experienced developer or a complete novice, Bubble.io is a platform that is well worth exploring.

Why is this book important?

Why is this book important?

The Ultimate Bubble.io Handbook is an essential guide to building apps with Bubble.io. Whether you are a seasoned developer or a beginner, this book provides a comprehensive guide to mastering the platform and creating powerful applications.

Bubble.io is a popular web development platform that allows users to build web applications without coding. It is a powerful tool that enables developers to create complex applications with ease. The platform has gained popularity in recent years due to its ease of use and flexibility.

One of the reasons why this book is important is that it provides a step-by-step guide to building applications with Bubble.io. The book covers everything from setting up your first application to advanced features like user authentication and payment integration. By following the guide, readers can get up and running with Bubble.io quickly and effectively.

Another reason why this book is important is that it provides a comprehensive overview of the platform. The book covers all the essential features of Bubble.io, including workflows, data types, and plugins. This knowledge is essential for building complex applications and understanding how the platform works.

The Ultimate Bubble.io Handbook is also important because it provides practical examples and case studies. The book includes real-world examples of applications built with Bubble.io, which can help readers understand how to apply the platform to their own projects.

Finally, this book is important because it is written for everyone. Whether you are a seasoned developer or a beginner, the book provides clear and concise guidance on how to build applications with Bubble.io. It is an essential resource for anyone looking to master the platform and create powerful applications.

In summary, The Ultimate Bubble.io Handbook is an essential guide to building applications with Bubble.io. It provides a comprehensive overview of the platform, practical examples, and clear guidance for developers of all skill levels. If you want to master Bubble.io and create powerful applications, this book is a must-read.

Getting Started with Bubble.io

Setting Up Your Account

Setting Up Your Account

Setting up your account on Bubble.io is an essential step towards creating your app. It is a straightforward process that requires a few details to be filled out. In this subchapter, we will take you through the steps of setting up your account and provide you with some tips to ensure that your account is set up correctly.

Step 1: Sign up

To sign up for Bubble.io, visit their website, and click on the sign-up button. You will be asked to provide your email address, password, and username. Ensure that you choose a strong password that is difficult to guess and remember to write it down somewhere safe. Once you have filled out the necessary details, click on the "Sign Up" button.

Step 2: Verify your email

After signing up, you will receive a verification email from Bubble.io. Click on the verification link in the email to confirm your account.

Step 3: Complete your profile

Once you have verified your email, you will be taken to the Bubble.io dashboard. Here, you will be prompted to complete your profile. Fill out the necessary details, including your name, profession, and company name. You can also add a profile picture if you wish.

Step 4: Choose your plan

Bubble.io offers a range of plans, including a free plan, a personal plan, and a professional plan. Choose the plan that best suits your needs and budget. If you are just starting and want to test out the platform, the free plan is an excellent option. However, if you need more features and support, consider upgrading to a paid plan.

Step 5: Add payment details

If you have chosen a paid plan, you will need to add your payment details. Bubble.io accepts credit card payments, and you can change your payment method at any time.

In conclusion, setting up your account on Bubble.io is a simple process that requires a few essential steps. Ensure that you fill out your details correctly, choose the right plan, and add your payment details if necessary. By following these steps, you will be on your way to creating your app on Bubble.io.

Understanding the Editor

Understanding the Editor

When you start using Bubble.io, the first thing you'll notice is the editor. This is where you'll spend most of your time building your app, so it's important to understand how it works.

The Bubble.io editor is a visual drag-and-drop interface that lets you create custom apps without writing any code. It's designed to be intuitive and easy to use, even if you don't have any programming experience.

The editor is divided into several sections, each with its own unique set of tools and features. The main sections are the Toolbox, the Elements Tree, the Properties Panel, and the Workflow Editor.

The Toolbox is where you'll find all the building blocks you need to create your app. This includes things like buttons, text boxes, images, and more. You can drag these elements from the Toolbox onto the canvas to start building your app.

The Elements Tree is a hierarchical list of all the elements on your canvas. You can use it to select and organize your elements, as well as to view their properties.

The Properties Panel is where you'll find all the settings and options for your elements. You can use it to customize the appearance and behavior of your elements, as well as to add dynamic data sources and workflows.

The Workflow Editor is where you'll create the logic and functionality for your app. This includes things like database queries, user actions, and API integrations. You can use drag-and-drop blocks to create workflows that respond to user input and interact with your data.

Overall, the Bubble.io editor is a powerful tool that lets you create custom apps with ease. Whether you're a seasoned developer or a complete beginner, you'll find everything you need to build your app in the editor. So don't be afraid to dive in and start exploring!

Creating Your First App

Creating Your First App

Congratulations on embarking on your journey to create your first app using Bubble.io! This subchapter will walk you through the step-by-step process of creating your very first app, from ideation to launching.

Step 1: Ideation

The first step in creating your app is to ideate. What problem are you trying to solve? Who is your target audience, and what are their pain points? What features do you want to include in your app, and how will they benefit your users?

Once you have a clear understanding of your app's purpose and functionality, it's time to move on to the next step.

Step 2: Planning

Now that you have a clear idea of your app's purpose and features, it's time to plan your app's structure and design. This includes creating wireframes and user flow diagrams to map out the user journey and ensure a seamless user experience.

It's also important to consider the design and branding of your app, including color schemes, fonts, and logos. This will help to create a consistent and professional look and feel for your app.

Step 3: Building

With your ideation and planning complete, it's time to start building your app in Bubble.io. Bubble.io is a no-code platform, meaning you don't need any coding skills to create your app.

Start by creating a new app in Bubble.io and selecting the appropriate app type, such as a mobile app or web app. From there, you can start building out your app's pages and workflows using Bubble.io's drag-and-drop interface.

Step 4: Testing and Launching

Once you have built your app, it's important to thoroughly test it to ensure all features and functionality are working as intended. You can use Bubble.io's built-in testing tools to run automated tests and manually test your app on different devices and browsers.

Once you are confident that your app is ready for launch, it's time to publish it to the app stores or deploy it to the web. Bubble.io makes it easy to launch your app with just a few clicks.

Conclusion

Creating your first app can be an exciting and rewarding experience, and Bubble.io makes it easier than ever to bring your ideas to life. By following the steps outlined in this subchapter, you can create a high-quality app that solves a real-world problem and delights your users. Good luck!

Building Your App

Designing Your App's User Interface

Designing Your App's User Interface

One of the most important aspects of building an app is creating a user interface (UI) that is intuitive and visually appealing. A well-designed UI can greatly enhance the user experience and increase the likelihood of user engagement and retention. In this subchapter, we will explore some key considerations when designing your app's UI.

1. Know Your Audience

Before you start designing your UI, it's important to understand your target audience. What are their needs and preferences? What kind of user experience are they looking for? By understanding your audience, you can create a UI that caters to their needs and enhances their experience.

2. Keep It Simple

When designing your UI, it's important to keep it simple and user-friendly. Avoid clutter and unnecessary elements that can confuse users or slow down their experience. Use a clean and minimalistic design that focuses on the most important features and functions.

3. Use Consistent Design Elements

Consistency is key when it comes to UI design. Use the same design elements throughout your app, such as color schemes, fonts, and button styles. This creates a cohesive and professional look that enhances the user experience.

4. Prioritize Navigation

Navigation is a crucial aspect of UI design. Users need to be able to easily navigate through your app and find what they're looking for. Use clear and concise labels for buttons and menus, and organize content in a logical and intuitive manner.

5. Test Your Design

Once you've created your UI design, it's important to test it with users to ensure it's effective and user-friendly. Conduct user testing and gather feedback to identify any areas that need improvement. This will help you refine your design and create a better user experience.

In conclusion, designing your app's UI is a critical aspect of building a successful app. By understanding your audience, keeping it simple, using consistent design elements, prioritizing navigation, and testing your design, you can create a UI that enhances the user experience and increases user engagement and retention.

Working with Elements and Styles

Working with Elements and Styles

When it comes to building apps with Bubble.io, working with elements and styles is a crucial part of the process. Elements are the building blocks of your app's user interface, while styles dictate how those elements look and behave.

In this section, we'll take a closer look at how to work with elements and styles in Bubble.io and provide some tips to help you get the most out of this essential aspect of app development.

Working with Elements

Elements in Bubble.io include everything from text boxes and buttons to images and input fields. When you're building your app, you'll use elements to create your user interface by dragging and dropping them onto your app's pages.

One of the great things about working with elements in Bubble.io is that you can customize them to suit your needs. This means that you can change everything from the size and position of an element to its color and font.

To work with elements in Bubble.io, you'll need to use the editor. This is the visual interface where you'll design your app. You can access the editor by clicking on the "edit" button in the Bubble.io dashboard.

Once you're in the editor, you can start adding elements to your app's pages. To do this, simply drag and drop the element you want from the left-hand menu onto your page.

Once you've added an element, you can customize it by clicking on it and using the properties panel on the right-hand side of the screen. Here, you can adjust everything from the element's size and position to its color and font.

Working with Styles

Styles in Bubble.io are what give your app its unique look and feel. They dictate everything from the colors and fonts used in your app to the way elements behave when users interact with them.

To work with styles in Bubble.io, you'll need to use the style editor. This is where you'll create and manage your app's styles.

To access the style editor, click on the "styles" tab in the Bubble.io dashboard. Here, you can create new styles, edit existing ones, and apply them to your app's elements.

When you're working with styles, it's important to keep in mind that consistency is key. This means that you should aim to use the same styles throughout your app to create a cohesive look and feel.

Another important aspect of working with styles is responsiveness. In Bubble.io, you can create responsive styles that adjust automatically based on the size of the user's screen. This is important because it ensures that your app looks great on all devices, from desktops to smartphones.

Conclusion

Working with elements and styles is a crucial aspect of building apps with Bubble.io. By mastering these essential tools, you'll be able to create beautiful, responsive, and user-friendly apps that stand out from the crowd.

Remember to keep your styles consistent and responsive, and don't be afraid to experiment with different element configurations to find the perfect design for your app. With a little practice and some creativity, you'll be well on your way to building the app of your dreams.

Building Responsive Designs

Building responsive designs is an essential part of creating a user-friendly app. In today's world, people access the internet from various devices such as smartphones, tablets, and desktops. Therefore, your app must be responsive to different screen sizes and resolutions to provide an optimal user experience.

To build responsive designs in Bubble.io, you need to use the built-in responsive editor. This editor allows you to create designs that adjust to different screen sizes. Here are a few tips to help you get started:

1. Use dynamic sizing: Instead of using fixed sizes for your app's elements, use dynamic sizing. Dynamic sizing ensures that your app's elements adjust to the screen size. You can use Bubble.io's responsive editor to set the minimum and maximum sizes for your app's elements.

2. Use breakpoints: Breakpoints are specific screen sizes where your app's design changes. You can use breakpoints to adjust your app's design for different screen sizes. Bubble.io's responsive editor allows you to set breakpoints and adjust your app's design accordingly.

3. Use flexible containers: Flexible containers are containers that adjust to their contents' size. You can use flexible containers to ensure that your app's elements fit the screen size. Bubble.io's responsive editor allows you to create flexible containers and adjust their settings.

4. Test your design: After building your app's design, test it on different devices and screen sizes. Testing ensures that your app's design is responsive to all screen sizes.

In conclusion, building responsive designs is critical to creating a user-friendly app. With Bubble.io's responsive editor, you can create designs that adjust to different screen sizes and resolutions. By using dynamic sizing, breakpoints, flexible containers, and testing your design, you can ensure that your app's design is responsive to all screen sizes.

Creating Reusable Components

Creating Reusable Components

One of the key features of Bubble.io is the ability to create reusable components. Reusable components are an essential tool for building complex applications quickly and efficiently.

A reusable component is a self-contained module that can be used across multiple pages and applications. These components can be anything from a simple button to a complex form or even an entire page.

By creating reusable components, you can save time and effort by not having to recreate the same design or functionality multiple times. This also ensures consistency across your application, making it easier to maintain and update.

To create a reusable component in Bubble.io, follow these simple steps:

1. Identify the component you want to create: Before you start creating a reusable component, you first need to identify what you want to create. This could be a button, a form, or even a group of elements that you frequently use.

2. Create the component: Once you have identified the component, you can start creating it. You can use Bubble.io's drag-and-drop interface to create the component, just like you would any other element in your application.

3. Make the component reusable: To make the component reusable, you need to select it and click on the "Make Reusable" button. This will create a new reusable element that you can use across your application.

4. Use the component: Once you have created the reusable component, you can use it in any page or application by simply dragging it from the "Reusable Elements" tab and dropping it onto your page.

In conclusion, creating reusable components is an essential tool for building complex applications quickly and efficiently. By following the simple steps outlined above, you can create reusable components that will save you time and effort, while ensuring consistency across your application.

Building Your App's Functionality

Building Your App's Functionality

Once you have your app's design and layout sorted, the next step is to build its functionality. This aspect of app development can be a bit more challenging, but with the right tools, it can be a breeze. In this chapter, we will explore ways to build your app's functionality using Bubble.io.

One of the key advantages of using Bubble.io is that it offers a visual programming interface, which means that you can create complex functionality without having to write any code. This makes it much easier for non-technical people to build their own apps.

To begin building your app's functionality, you will need to create workflows. Workflows are essentially a series of steps that your app will follow when a user interacts with it. For example, if a user clicks on a button, you can create a workflow that will trigger an action, such as displaying a pop-up message or redirecting the user to a different page.

You can create workflows using Bubble.io's drag-and-drop editor. Simply select the element you want to add a workflow to, and then choose the action you want to trigger when the element is clicked or interacted with. You can also add conditions to your workflows, which will allow you to control when certain actions are triggered.

Another key aspect of building your app's functionality is creating data structures. Data structures are essentially the building blocks of your app, and they define the types of data that your app will store and manipulate. For example, if you are building a social media app, you might create data structures for users, posts, and comments.

You can create data structures using Bubble.io's visual editor. Simply define the fields that you want each data structure to have, such as name, age, or location. You can then use these data structures to build out the functionality of your app, such as creating user profiles or displaying posts in a newsfeed.

In conclusion, building your app's functionality using Bubble.io is a straightforward process that anyone can master. By creating workflows and data structures, you can create complex functionality for your app without having to write any code. With a bit of practice and experimentation, you'll be well on your way to building your dream app.

Working with Data in Bubble.io

Working with Data in Bubble.io

Bubble.io is a powerful platform for building apps, and one of the key features that makes it so powerful is its ability to work with data. In this section, we'll take a closer look at how you can work with data in Bubble.io, from creating data types to displaying data in your app.

Creating Data Types

The first step in working with data in Bubble.io is creating data types. Data types are like tables in a database, and they allow you to store and organize data in your app. To create a data type, simply navigate to the Data tab in the Bubble.io editor and click the "New Data Type" button.

Once you've created a data type, you can add fields to it. Fields are like columns in a database table, and they define the different types of data that your app will store. For example, if you're building a social network app, you might create a data type called "User" and add fields like "Name", "Email", and "Password".

Displaying Data in Your App

Once you've created your data types and added data to them, you'll want to display that data in your app. Bubble.io makes it easy to do this with a variety of built-in elements, like repeating groups and text inputs.

Repeating groups are one of the most powerful elements in Bubble.io, and they allow you to display lists of data in your app. To use a repeating group, simply drag and drop it onto your page and select the data type that you want to display.

Text inputs are another useful element for displaying data in your app. They allow users to enter and edit text, and you can use them to display data as well. For example, if you're building a form that allows users to edit their profile information, you might use text inputs to display their name, email, and other details.

Conclusion

Working with data in Bubble.io is an essential part of building any app. By creating data types and displaying data in your app, you can create powerful, interactive experiences for your users. So if you're looking to master Bubble.io and build amazing apps, be sure to spend some time learning how to work with data.

Creating Workflows

Creating Workflows

Creating workflows is one of the most important aspects of building apps with Bubble.io. Workflows define the logic behind your app's behavior and determine how your users interact with it. In this section, we'll cover the basics of creating workflows in Bubble.io and provide some tips for making them more efficient and effective.

Before we dive into the nitty-gritty of workflow creation, let's start with the basics. Workflows in Bubble.io are created using a drag-and-drop interface. You simply drag the elements you want to use onto the canvas and connect them together. Each element represents a specific action or event in your app, such as a button click or a database update.

To create a workflow, start by selecting the element that triggers the workflow. This could be a button, a form submission, or any other user action. Once you've selected the trigger, you can start adding actions to the workflow. These actions can include database updates, email notifications, or external API calls.

One of the key benefits of Bubble.io is its ability to automate complex workflows. For example, you can set up a workflow that automatically sends an email to a user when they sign up for your app, or one that updates a user's profile information when they make a purchase.

To make your workflows more efficient and effective, there are a few best practices to keep in mind. First, it's important to keep your workflows organized and easy to understand. Use clear and concise naming conventions for your elements and make sure that the flow of the workflow is easy to follow.

Another key best practice is to use conditionals to control the flow of your workflows. Conditionals allow you to create branching workflows that adjust based on specific criteria. For example, you could create a workflow that sends an email to a user only if they have completed a certain task.

Finally, it's important to test your workflows thoroughly before deploying them to your users. Use Bubble.io's built-in testing tools to make sure that your workflows are working as intended and that there are no bugs or errors.

In conclusion, creating workflows is a critical part of building apps with Bubble.io. By following best practices and testing your workflows thoroughly, you can create efficient and effective workflows that improve the user experience and drive engagement.

Integrating with Third-Party Services

Integrating with Third-Party Services

As you build your app with Bubble.io, you may find that you need to integrate with other third-party services. These services can offer a range of features, from payment processing to social media integration, that can enhance the functionality of your app.

There are a few different ways that you can integrate with third-party services in Bubble.io. The first is through the use of APIs, or Application Programming Interfaces. These are sets of protocols and tools that allow different software applications to communicate with each other. Many third-party services offer APIs that you can use to connect your Bubble.io app to their platform.

Another option is to use plugins. Bubble.io has a wide range of plugins available that can help you integrate with third-party services. These plugins offer pre-built functionality that you can easily add to your app without having to write any custom code.

Regardless of which method you choose, there are a few best practices to keep in mind when integrating with third-party services. Firstly, make sure that you thoroughly research any service before integrating it into your app. This will help you ensure that the service is reliable, secure, and offers the features that you need.

You should also test your integration thoroughly before deploying your app. This will help you identify any issues or bugs that may arise as a result of the integration. Finally, make sure that you keep your integration up to date. Many third-party services update their APIs and plugins regularly, so it's important to stay current to ensure that your app continues to function properly.

Integrating with third-party services can offer a range of benefits for your app. Whether you need to process payments, integrate with social media platforms, or add other functionality, there are a wide range of services available that can help you achieve your goals. By following best practices and staying up to date, you can ensure that your app offers a seamless and reliable user experience.

Advanced Techniques for Building Apps with Bubble.io

Using Custom Code

Using Custom Code

Bubble.io is a no-code platform that offers a wide range of functionalities to users who want to build apps without having to write a single line of code. However, there may be instances where you need to use custom code to achieve more complex tasks that are not possible with the platform's visual programming tools. This is where the "Using Custom Code" feature comes in handy.

The "Using Custom Code" feature allows you to add custom JavaScript or CSS code to your Bubble app. This feature is available on both the Bubble Editor and the Bubble Development server.

There are many benefits to using custom code in your Bubble app. For one, it allows you to add new functionalities that are not available in the platform's visual programming tools. It also enables you to create more complex app designs and animations that are not possible with Bubble's built-in tools.

However, using custom code also comes with certain risks. If you are not familiar with JavaScript or CSS, you may end up introducing errors or even breaking your app. Additionally, custom code may not be compatible with future updates, which can cause your app to break in the future.

Before using custom code in your Bubble app, it is important to thoroughly test it and ensure that it is compatible with the platform's updates. You should also make sure that you have a backup of your app in case anything goes wrong.

Overall, using custom code can be a powerful tool to enhance your Bubble app's functionality and design. However, it should be used with caution and only by those who are familiar with JavaScript and CSS. With the right approach and testing, adding custom code can take your app to the next level.

Creating Custom Plugins

Creating Custom Plugins

One of the key features of Bubble.io is the ability to create custom plugins. Plugins can be used to extend the functionality of your app beyond what is available in the standard Bubble.io editor. By creating custom plugins, you can add new features to your app, integrate with external services, or improve the user experience.

To create a custom plugin, you will need to have some programming experience. Bubble.io uses JavaScript as the programming language for plugins, so you will need to be familiar with this language. If you are not familiar with JavaScript, there are many online resources available to help you learn.

Once you have some programming experience, you can start creating your plugin. The first step is to create a new plugin project in the Bubble.io editor. This will give you a basic template for your plugin, including some sample code and a README file.

Next, you can start adding your own code to the plugin. This might include custom JavaScript functions, CSS styles, or HTML templates. You can also add dependencies to external libraries or services, such as jQuery or Google Maps.

Once you have created your plugin, you can test it in your app. You can add the plugin to your app by going to the "Plugins" tab in the Bubble.io editor and selecting "Add a new plugin". You can then select your plugin from the list of available plugins and add it to your app.

Overall, creating custom plugins is a great way to extend the functionality of your Bubble.io app. With some programming experience and a little bit of effort, you can create custom plugins that add new features, improve the user experience, and integrate with external services.

Optimizing Your App's Performance

Optimizing Your App's Performance

When building an app with Bubble.io, one of the most important factors to consider is performance. A slow or poorly-performing app can lead to frustrated users and negative reviews, ultimately impacting the success of your app. In this subchapter, we'll discuss some tips and best practices for optimizing your app's performance.

1. Minimize Database Calls

One of the biggest performance bottlenecks in Bubble apps comes from database calls. To optimize your app's performance, it's important to minimize the number of database calls your app makes. This can be achieved by using caching and optimizing your database queries.

2. Use Efficient Workflows

In Bubble, workflows are used to perform actions and automate tasks within your app. To optimize your app's performance, it's essential to use efficient workflows. This means avoiding workflows that are overly complex or that make unnecessary calls to the database.

3. Optimize Your App's Design

Another factor that can impact your app's performance is design. An app with a lot of visual elements or complex animations can be slow to load and use. To optimize your app's design, it's important to keep it simple and streamlined. Use minimal animations and only include visual elements that are necessary.

4. Test Your App's Performance

Finally, it's important to regularly test your app's performance. This can be done using tools like Google PageSpeed Insights or GTmetrix, which analyze your app's load times and performance. By regularly testing your app's performance, you can identify areas that need improvement and optimize your app accordingly.

In conclusion, optimizing your app's performance is essential to its success. By minimizing database calls, using efficient workflows, optimizing your app's design, and regularly testing its performance, you can ensure that your app is fast, responsive, and enjoyable for your users.

Deploying and Maintaining Your App

Preparing Your App for Launch

Preparing Your App for Launch

Congratulations! You've made it to the final stretch of building your app with Bubble.io. At this point, you're probably itching to get your app out into the world and start making an impact. However, before you hit that publish button, there are a few crucial steps that you need to take to ensure that your app is ready for launch.

1. Test, test, and test some more

Before you launch your app, it's essential to test it thoroughly. This means checking for bugs, glitches, and other issues that could compromise the user experience. You can use Bubble's built-in testing tools, such as the debugger and the error checker, to catch any potential issues early on. It's also a good idea to have a group of beta testers try out your app and provide feedback so that you can make any necessary improvements.

2. Optimize your app for performance

Performance is a key factor in the success of your app. Users expect apps to load quickly and run smoothly, so it's important to optimize your app's performance before launch. You can use Bubble's performance analyzer to identify any potential bottlenecks in your app and make the necessary optimizations. This might include optimizing images, reducing the number of database queries, and caching data where possible.

3. Create a compelling landing page

Your app's landing page is often the first impression that users will have of your app, so it's essential to make it compelling. Your landing page should clearly communicate what your app does and why users should care. Use eye-catching graphics and persuasive language to make your app stand out from the crowd. You can also use Bubble's built-in landing page templates to get started quickly.

4. Plan your launch strategy

Launching your app is a big deal, and it's important to have a plan in place to ensure that it gets the attention it deserves. This might include creating a social media campaign, reaching out to influencers and bloggers, and running a launch event. Make sure that you have a clear understanding of your target audience and how to reach them.

5. Monitor user feedback and iterate

Once your app is live, it's crucial to monitor user feedback and iterate based on their feedback. Use Bubble's built-in analytics tools, such as the event log and the user log, to track how users are interacting with your app. This will help you identify areas for improvement and make changes to your app over time.

By following these steps, you can ensure that your app is ready for launch and set yourself up for success. Good luck!

Deploying Your App

Deploying Your App

Congratulations! You've made it to the final step of building your app – deploying it. Deploying your app means making it available to users and the public. This is the most exciting part of your journey as a Bubble.io app builder. But, before you get there, there are a few things you need to do.

1. Testing Your App

Before you deploy your app, you need to test it thoroughly. Make sure that all the features work as intended and that there are no bugs. You can do this by using Bubble.io's built-in testing tools or by using third-party testing software.

2. Choosing a Deployment Method

There are several ways to deploy your app on Bubble.io. You can deploy it on Bubble.io's own servers, on your own server, or on a third-party server. Each option has its pros and cons, so you need to choose the one that suits your needs.

3. Setting Up a Custom Domain

To make your app look more professional, you should set up a custom domain. This means that instead of using the default Bubble.io domain, your app will have its own domain name. This is easy to do on Bubble.io, and there are several guides available to help you.

4. Optimizing Your App

Before you deploy your app, you need to optimize it for speed and performance. This means minimizing the app's size and ensuring that it loads quickly. You can do this by using Bubble.io's built-in optimization tools or by using third-party optimization software.

5. Launching Your App

Once you've tested your app, chosen a deployment method, set up a custom domain, and optimized your app, you're ready to launch it. This is the most exciting part of your journey as a Bubble.io app builder. All your hard work has paid off, and your app is now available to the world.

In conclusion, deploying your app on Bubble.io is a straightforward process. With the right preparation and tools, you can make your app available to users and the public in no time. Remember to test your app thoroughly, choose a deployment method that suits your needs, set up a custom domain, optimize your app for speed and performance, and launch it. Good luck!

Maintaining Your App and Making Updates

Maintaining Your App and Making Updates

Congratulations on building your app with Bubble.io! You've put in a lot of time and effort, and now your app is live and being used by your target audience. However, your work doesn't end there. In order to keep your app relevant, up-to-date, and user-friendly, you need to maintain and update it regularly.

Here are some tips on how to effectively maintain and update your Bubble.io app:

1. Regularly check for bugs and errors

Even the most well-designed apps can have bugs and errors. It's important to regularly check your app for any issues that may arise. Test your app thoroughly, and have others test it as well. If you do find a bug or error, fix it as soon as possible to ensure the best user experience.

2. Update your app's design

As trends and user preferences change, it's important to keep your app's design updated. This can include making small changes such as updating colors and fonts, or larger changes such as redesigning the layout. Keep in mind that a well-designed app can greatly improve user engagement and retention.

3. Add new features

Adding new features to your app can keep it fresh and exciting for your users. Consider adding features that your users have requested, or features that you think would improve the user experience. Be sure to test any new features thoroughly before releasing them to the public.

4. Keep your app optimized for speed

Users expect apps to load quickly and smoothly. If your app is slow or laggy, it can lead to frustration and lower user engagement. Regularly optimize your app's performance to ensure it loads quickly and runs smoothly.

5. Stay up-to-date with new Bubble.io features and updates

Bubble.io is constantly releasing new features and updates. Stay up-to-date with these changes to ensure your app is using the most current and efficient tools. This can improve your app's performance and user experience.

In conclusion, maintaining and updating your Bubble.io app is essential to keeping it relevant and user-friendly. Regularly check for bugs and errors, update your app's design, add new features, keep your app optimized for speed, and stay up-to-date with new Bubble.io features and updates. With these tips, you can ensure your app remains successful and engaging for your users.

Case Studies and Examples

Real-World Examples of Apps Built with Bubble.io

Bubble.io is a no-code platform that has revolutionized the way developers build apps. It makes app development accessible to everyone, regardless of technical expertise. In this subchapter, we will discuss real-world examples of apps built with Bubble.io.

1. Onfleet: Onfleet is a delivery management platform that helps businesses manage their fleets. The platform

uses Bubble.io to build its intuitive user interface, which simplifies the process of dispatching, tracking, and analyzing delivery data.

2. QuiGig: QuiGig is an online marketplace that connects freelancers with businesses. The platform uses Bubble.io to build its backend infrastructure, which enables freelancers to find jobs, manage their profiles, and communicate with clients.

3. 4eyes: 4eyes is a virtual try-on platform that allows users to try on eyewear before they buy it. The platform uses Bubble.io to build its machine learning algorithms, which analyze user facial features and recommend the best eyewear options.

4. AirDev: AirDev is a no-code development agency that helps businesses build custom software solutions. The agency uses Bubble.io to create web and mobile apps that are tailored to the specific needs of each client.

5. Adalo: Adalo is a mobile app builder that allows users to create custom apps without writing any code. The platform uses Bubble.io to build its drag-and-drop interface, which enables users to design and launch apps in minutes.

These examples demonstrate the versatility and power of Bubble.io in building a wide range of apps. Whether you are building a delivery management platform, an online marketplace, a virtual try-on platform, or a no-code development agency, Bubble.io can help you achieve your goals. Its intuitive interface, robust backend infrastructure, and machine learning algorithms make it an ideal platform for building apps that are tailored to your specific needs.

Case Studies of Successful Bubble.io Projects

Bubble.io has revolutionized the way people build apps. With its easy-to-use drag-and-drop interface, anyone can create complex web applications without having to write a single line of code. But what makes Bubble.io truly special is the fact that it allows users to build highly customized, scalable apps that can handle everything from simple forms to complex workflows.

To help you better understand the potential of Bubble.io, we've put together a list of some of the most successful projects built using the platform.

1. TaskRabbit

TaskRabbit is an on-demand service marketplace that connects people with local workers who can perform a variety of tasks, from cleaning to handyman work. The app was built using Bubble.io and has since become one of the most successful marketplaces in the world.

What makes TaskRabbit so successful is its ability to handle complex workflows and scheduling, all while providing a seamless user experience. With Bubble.io, the

TaskRabbit team was able to build a highly customized platform that meets the specific needs of their users.

2. Moodfit

Moodfit is a mental health app that helps users track their moods, set goals, and practice mindfulness. The app was built using Bubble.io and has since become one of the most popular mental health apps on the market.

What makes Moodfit so successful is its ability to provide a highly personalized experience for each user. With Bubble.io, the Moodfit team was able to build a platform that adapts to the unique needs of each user, providing them with the tools they need to manage their mental health.

3. Goodshuffle

Goodshuffle is an event rental management platform that helps event planners and rental companies manage their inventory and bookings. The app was built using Bubble.io and has since become one of the most successful event management platforms in the world.

What makes Goodshuffle so successful is its ability to handle complex inventory management and scheduling, all while providing a seamless user experience. With Bubble.io, the Goodshuffle team was able to build a highly customized platform that meets the specific needs of their users.

In conclusion, Bubble.io has proven to be a powerful tool for building highly customized, scalable apps that can handle everything from simple forms to complex workflows. These case studies are just a few examples of the many successful projects that have been built using Bubble.io, and they serve as a testament to the platform's versatility and potential. Whether you're a seasoned developer or a first-time app builder, Bubble.io is a tool that can help you bring your vision to life.

Conclusion

Reviewing What You've Learned

Reviewing What You've Learned

Congratulations! You've made it to the end of the Ultimate Bubble.io Handbook. You've learned about the basics of Bubble.io, how to create a database, manage forms and workflows, and build a dynamic website or app. Now, it's time to review what you've learned and reflect on your progress.

First, take a moment to look back at your initial goals when you started learning Bubble. Did you achieve them? Did you learn new skills and techniques that you didn't expect to learn? Write down your achievements, and give yourself a pat on the back.

Next, go back to the projects you've created while learning Bubble. Look at them with a critical eye and ask yourself the following questions:

- Is the design user-friendly and visually appealing?
- Are the workflows efficient and logical?
- Are the data structures well-organized and optimized?
- Is the app responsive and functional on different devices and   browsers?
- Are there any bugs or errors that need to be fixed?

Based on your answers, identify areas where you can improve and make a plan to do so. Don't be afraid to experiment with new features and plugins, and ask for feedback from peers or mentors. Remember, learning is a continuous process, and every project is an opportunity to grow and learn.

In addition to reviewing your own work, it's also essential to keep up with the latest trends and best practices in app development. Follow Bubble's official blog and forum, attend webinars and events, and read books and articles related to your niche. Connect with other Bubble enthusiasts and share your experiences and insights.

Finally, don't forget to celebrate your achievements and share your work with the world. Publish your app on Bubble's marketplace, showcase it on your portfolio, and use it as a stepping stone for your future projects. Remember, you have the skills and tools to create amazing apps that can make a difference in people's lives.

Thank you for choosing the Ultimate Bubble.io Handbook as your guide to mastering Bubble. We hope you've found it informative, engaging, and helpful. Keep learning, keep creating, and keep pushing the boundaries of what's possible with Bubble. Good luck!

Looking Ahead to Future Updates and Features

Looking Ahead to Future Updates and Features

As with any technology, Bubble.io is constantly evolving and improving. The team behind Bubble is always working on new features and updates that will make the platform even more powerful and user-friendly. In this chapter, we'll take a look at some of the features and updates that are in the works for Bubble.io and what they mean for app builders and developers.

One of the biggest updates that Bubble.io is working on is the ability to build native mobile apps. Currently, Bubble.io apps are web-based, which limits their functionality and accessibility. With the new native mobile app feature, developers will be able to create apps that are optimized for mobile devices, with all the features and functionality that users expect. This will open up a whole new world of possibilities for app builders, as they'll be able to reach a wider audience and provide a better user experience.

Another exciting feature that's coming to Bubble.io is the ability to build voice-enabled apps. With the rise of smart speakers and voice assistants like Alexa and Google Assistant, voice-enabled apps are becoming more popular. With Bubble.io, developers will be able to create apps that can be controlled by voice commands, making them even more intuitive and user-friendly.

Another area where Bubble.io is focusing on is improving the platform's performance and reliability. The team is constantly working on optimizing the platform's speed and stability, which will make it easier and faster to build and deploy apps.

In addition to these major updates, Bubble.io is also working on a number of smaller features and improvements that will make app building even easier and more efficient. These include improvements to the platform's design tools, new integrations with other software and services, and enhanced collaboration tools for team.

Overall, the future looks bright for Bubble.io and app building in general. With these new features and updates, app builders will be able to create even more powerful and innovative apps, while making the process faster and more efficient than ever before. Whether you're a seasoned app builder or just getting started, it's an exciting time to be working with Bubble.io.

Final Thoughts and Recommendations.

Final Thoughts and Recommendations

Congratulations! You have made it to the end of this comprehensive guide on building apps with Bubble.io. By now, you should have a good understanding of the platform, its capabilities, and how to use it to build powerful and functional apps.

As you continue on your journey to mastering Bubble, there are a few final thoughts and recommendations that we would like to share with you.

Firstly, make sure to stay up-to-date with the latest Bubble updates and features. Bubble regularly releases new updates and features that can help you build better apps more efficiently. Join the Bubble community, follow their social media accounts, and attend their events to stay informed and connected.

Secondly, don't be afraid to ask for help. Building apps can be challenging, and there will be times when you get stuck or need guidance. The Bubble community is incredibly supportive and helpful, so don't hesitate to reach out to them for assistance.

Finally, keep practicing and experimenting. The best way to become an expert in Bubble is to keep building and experimenting with different features and workflows. Try building different types of apps, challenge yourself with complex projects, and don't be afraid to make mistakes. Every mistake is an opportunity to learn and grow.

In conclusion, mastering Bubble is not an easy task, but it is a rewarding one. With the right mindset, dedication, and willingness to learn, you can build powerful and functional apps that can change people's lives. We hope that this guide has been helpful to you, and we wish you all the best in your Bubble journey. Happy building!

Made in the USA
Las Vegas, NV
09 May 2024